Faithful Against Torture

Faithful Against Torture

**Citizens for Global Solutions
(Reissued September 2009)**

iUniverse, Inc.
New York   Bloomington

Faithful Against Torture

iUniverse books may be ordered through booksellers or by contacting:

iUniverse
1663 Liberty Drive
Bloomington, IN 47403
www.iuniverse.com
1-800-Authors (1-800-288-4677)

Because of the dynamic nature of the Internet, any Web addresses or links contained in this book may have changed since publication and may no longer be valid. The views expressed in this work are solely those of the author and do not necessarily reflect the views of the publisher, and the publisher hereby disclaims any responsibility for them.

ISBN: 978-1-4401-0849-5 (pbk)
ISBN: 978-1-4401-0850-1 (ebk)

Printed in the United States of America

iUniverse rev. date: 9/18/2009

Acknowledgments:

Cory Smith, Raj Purohit and Bill Mefford, who co-directed the project, would like to thank the authors who generously shared their thoughts and ideas for this publication. Thanks go as well to the General Board of Church and Society at The United Methodist Church of Washington, DC, where Bill Mefford serves as the Director of Civil and Human Rights. Special thanks to Tom Moran and Jen Maceyko for their assistance in editing and production. Citizens for Global Solutions would like to thank the JEHT Foundation for its generous support.

Contents

Introduction to the 2009 Edition

The essays in this collection were written in 2008, before the more recent revelation of information about the interrogation techniques employed by the United States during the Bush Administration and before the Obama Administration had taken its initial steps in addressing questions related to the conduct of torture by the United States.

When questions about torture initially arose after the establishment of the detention facility in Guantanamo Bay, the public debate on torture could hardly be joined in earnest because secrecy surrounded many of the most salient facts and circumstances. The public is now learning specific information about exactly what was done, to whom, and when. The American people are now coming to appreciate that these things were done in our name, on our behalf, and with the claim of our consent.

The debate in the United States on the use of torture is really only beginning.

Faithful Against Torture provides invaluable insights and a solid foundation for considering the questions relating to the use of torture by our government. Recognizing the durability of these essays and their relevance to the evolving public debate, we are reissuing this volume.

To date the public debate over the use of torture by the United States has been remarkably superficial. In the media it is almost as if fundamental questions about torture are being considered for the first time. Some commentators act as if the so-called "ticking time bomb" scenario is novel and therefore perplexing, as if serious ethical thinkers had not already wrestled for centuries with the dilemma of whether "ends" always justify "means."

Elected officials, editorial writers, television commentators, and today's ubiquitous "bloggers" have waded into this debate with "shoot from the hip" talking points, rarely acknowledging the conclusions of the long lines of philosophers and theologians who have carefully and rigorously considered the arguments for and against torture. Questions about torture have implications beyond the next news cycle.

Faithful Against Torture springs from a modest proposition: That in considering torture, a question that draws on our deepest values and whose answer defines our nation, we should be informed by our religious traditions and the thinking of our religious leaders. In reading these essays, the discussion is elevated above the technical definition of torture or the question of whether torture "works."

"Faithful" from St. Thomas Aquinas to Dietrich Bonhoeffer have offered an ecumenical basis for the denunciation of torture. Centered on respect for the Almighty, based on respect for the dignity of each human being, based on calls for compassion and justice, as well as appeals to the rule of law, the "faithful" have condemned torture. These essays explain that and put that condemnation in context.

As additional facts are made known, as we grapple with accountability for what we have done, as we establish rules to govern ourselves and our leaders in the future, the essays in this volume set forth timeless principles that refresh our thinking and remind us that we are not the first to confront these issues. And, unfortunately, we will not be the last.

Robert A. Enholm
Executive Vice President
Citizens for Global Solutions
Washington, DC

PREFACE

Why Are People of Faith Working to End U.S.-Sponsored Torture?

It is safe to say that millions of people of faith believe strongly that the U.S. policies and practices of torture and cruel, inhuman and degrading treatment are wrong. Tens of thousands are involved with the National Religious Campaign Against Torture, an organization created in January 2006, that has over 150 religious organizations as members. These member groups include diverse faith traditions: evangelical Christians, mainline Protestants, Roman Catholics, Orthodox Christians, Quakers, Buddhists, Unitarians, Muslims, Jews, and Sikhs.

Notwithstanding points of theological difference, these groups have made a commitment to work together to end U.S.-sponsored torture. They understand that torture is a moral issue because morality requires good behavior.

Governments are not behaving well when they engage in the torture and cruel, inhuman and degrading treatment of detainees, or when the standards of the U.S. Army Field Manual are not required of the CIA or contractors. Governments are not behaving well when the ancient human right of habeas corpus is denied. Governments are not behaving well when there are secret prisons or detainees are sent to other countries known to use torture in their interrogation methods.

Why are people from these diverse faith groups in agreement about the immorality of torture and making a commitment to work together to end U.S.-sponsored torture? These religious nations share a basic understanding and affirmation of the inherent dignity of each individual which includes:

- A conviction that all human beings are endowed with a basic dignity. Most of these religions express that belief by saying that all individuals are created in the image of God. The dignity that all people possess requires that everyone should be honored and treated well. People of faith are called to be faithful and constant in their defense of each individual's dignity and humanity.

- Most religions require a variant of what is commonly referred to as "The Golden Rule": that which you would not want done to yourself, do not do to another. Many policymakers have concluded that the golden rule is helpful in examining interrogation practices. The United States should only allow the CIA and other agencies to engage in interrogation techniques that we would agree could be used on our soldiers and personnel.

- People of faith are called to compassion - to care for people who are degraded or hurt or abused. Because compassion leads religious people to work to end the causes of the abuse and degradation, thousands are engaged in the work to end U.S.-sponsored torture.

- People of faith are called to pursue justice to assure that all people are treated fairly - as Martin Luther King once noted, "Injustice anywhere is a threat to justice everywhere." At its heart, torture is an injustice. No one deserves to be treated in such a humiliating and degrading way.

- People of faith are called to hospitality - to welcome those who are marginalized and ostracized. They are hospitable even to those who are of a different religion, a different ethnic group or a different nationality. They are even called to be welcoming to those who are enemies.

- People of faith are called to make peace - to facilitate reconciliation and to create a culture of peace. Torturing not only makes enemies with those who are tortured, it diminishes our nation in the eyes of our allies and other countries of the world.

Religious institutions are called to embody these values and to engage in these tasks. Religious traditions emphasize ethical behavior as a witness to their faith. Because of the moral authority these bring, religion can provide leadership to these issues in society as a whole. They also provide leadership in secular society, playing an important role in influencing issues of morality. Furthermore, the infrastructure that they provide supports the millions of people who covet justice and peace for all of God's creation.

Alexis de Tocqueville, the French historian and observer of 19th century America, said that "America is great because America is good. If America ceases to be good, America will cease to be great." If we want a great nation, we must work to assure that we have a good one. Instead of bad behavior, people of faith work to assure that torture and all denials of human rights are replaced with guarantees of respect, dignity, justice and fairness.

This book is a helpful collection of essays by people of faith who dig deeply into their own traditions and apply the wisdom of their faiths to the issue of torture. Religious traditions have a great deal to say about torture and cruel, inhuman and degrading treatment of prisoners. This volume captures well the insights and teachings of various faith traditions. You are urged to read these essays and share them with others in your congregation and faith communities.

Rev. Richard L. Killmer
Executive Director, National Religious Campaign Against Torture
Washington, DC

The Catholic Position on Torture: It Is NEVER Justified - *Mea Culpa!*

Like any human emotion, fear can be a useful sign, warning us of a real danger. But fear that is not balanced with a well grounded and fully life-giving and life-promoting response is merely life-sapping paranoia and terror that madly drives people to do outrageous and immoral things. Such is the state of the United States as a moral agent in the world concerning torture in the present day. Reinforced daily by the Bush administration's fear-engendering post-9/11 world "spin" on the daily news, Bishop John H. Ricard of the U.S. Catholic Bishops' International Policy Committee observed: "Some people feel the situation is out of control. They feel a vulnerability and a temptation to respond in kind. We have to resist that."

As a nation, we have allowed ourselves to be ruled by fear! We have forgotten not only the political wisdom of FDR—"The only thing we have to fear is fear itself!"—but most tragically, we have lost track of the moral deficiency of fear! Without a doubt, the traditional values of America and America's major religious traditions have been ignored, and in its place, fear has been manipulated via the purportedly well reasoned logic (read: illogic) of the Bush administration allegedly justifying the need to contravene the prohibitions of the Geneva Conventions and the United Nations Declarations prohibiting torture.

Significantly, fear was identified by the medieval moralists as one of the impediments to sound moral reasoning and judgment (along with ignorance, passion, force, prejudice, mental illness, bad habits, and personality disorder). The kind of fear that destroys moral sensibilities on this scale is very new to U.S. believers. But the medieval moralists also held that fear was something that could be overcome with additional effort on the part of the moral agent (Timothy E. O'Connell, *Making Disciples,* 33-34).

The Roman Catholic Church's position on torture opens a path to the only way out of this state of fear, namely that we as a nation with God's help, act justly—even toward our "enemies"! In so doing, *we,* not *they,* take control of the moral status of our acts and in so doing regain our moral fidelity and credibility concerning human and civil rights and the democratic values we proclaim and promote, and which supposedly motivated us to take on the "enemy" in the first place!

Briefly put, torture is intrinsically evil and an absolute synthetic formal moral norm that prohibits its practice universally and unconditionally. This prohibition holds particularly against torture as it is being promoted in the context of the Bush Administration's War on Terror and in light of the recent debates concerning the definition of what constitutes torture. I also suggest that, in addition to promoting the traditional theological and ethical explanations of this position, it is necessary for us as a nation (as well as the Catholic Church and other religious groups) to attend to the affective dimension of the moral formation of believers and citizens if the United States is to not become mired down by its growing reputation as the world's most hypocritical and hated nation.

I. The Sources and the Teaching – *Cognitio Speculativa*

All Catholic teaching concerning torture flows from divine revelation of the most fundamental identity of each human person as one created in the image and likeness of God (Gen. 1: 26-3; 2:4-7). This identity endows each human person with an inviolable dignity that cannot be dishonored, debased, despoiled, desecrated, manipulated, or sullied in any way. There is *no* justifiable reason to assault this dignity. Torture, without question, directly violates both the human dignity of the victim and the perpetrator. Torture idolatrously places one human being over another, who, by inflicting horrendous pain and agony, imprints on the victim—physically, psychologically, and spiritually—a redefinition of her or his being as a worthless object. This position was reasserted in a document that bears the Church's highest authority, the Second Vatican Council's *Gaudium et spes* §§ 27-28.

II. Respect for Bodily Integrity

The *Catechism of the Catholic Church* spells out the absolute prohibition against torture in terms of protection of the bodily integrity of the human person.

> **2297** […] *Torture* which uses physical or moral violence to extract confessions, punish the guilty, frighten opponents, or satisfy hatred is contrary to respect for the person and for human dignity. Except when performed for strictly therapeutic medical reasons, directly intended *amputations, mutilations,* and *sterilizations* performed on innocent persons are against the moral law (cf. DS 3722).

> **2298** In times past, cruel practices were commonly used by legitimate governments to maintain law and order, often without protest from the Pastors of the Church, who themselves adopted in their own tribunals the prescriptions of Roman law concerning torture. Regrettable as these facts are, the Church always taught the duty of clemency and mercy. She forbade clerics to shed blood. In recent times it has become evident that these cruel practices were neither necessary for public order nor in conformity with the legitimate rights of the human person. On the contrary, these practices led to ones even more degrading. It is necessary to work for their abolition. We must pray for the victims and their tormentors.

Here in §2297, the Catholic Church recognizes once again the God-given dignity of each person. However, in §2298 the Church's honest and remorseful voice is heard, repenting and grieving its past egregious and horrific violations of its own teaching concerning torture (in the Crusades and the Inquisition of the medieval period, for example). Thus, the Church not only speaks from divine authority but also with the authority of the experience of having tried to justify torture and use it for a "good cause"— but found that such an approach is equally morally wanting.

The Compendium of Social Doctrine of the Catholic Church §404 states the following in the context of the discussion of rightful political authority:

404 *The activity of offices charged with establishing criminal responsibility, which is always personal in character, must strive to be a meticulous search for truth and must be conducted in full respect for the dignity and rights of the human person;* this means guaranteeing the rights of the guilty as well as those of the innocent. The juridical principle by which punishment cannot be inflicted if a crime has not first been proven must be borne in mind.

In carrying out investigations, the regulation against the use of torture, even in the case of serious crimes, must be strictly observed: "Christ's disciple refuses every recourse to such methods, which nothing could justify and in which the dignity of man is as much debased in his torturer as in the torturer's victim." International juridical instruments concerning human rights correctly indicate a prohibition against torture as a principle that cannot be contravened under any circumstances.

Likewise ruled out is "the use of detention for the sole purpose of trying to obtain significant information for the trial." Moreover, it must be ensured that "trials are conducted swiftly: their excessive length is becoming intolerable for citizens and results in a real injustice."

Officials of the court are especially called to exercise due discretion in their investigations so as not to violate the rights of the accused to confidentiality and in order not to undermine the principle of the presumption of innocence. Since even judges can make mistakes, it is proper that the law provide for suitable compensation for victims of judicial errors. (Footnotes omitted).

In the context of defining the morality of any human action, *The Catechism of the Catholic Church* also specifies that:

1759 An evil action cannot be justified by reference to a good intention (cf. St. Thomas Aquinas, *Dec. praec.* 6). The end does not justify the means.

In the U.S. context, the Catholic Church has made it explicit that torture is an intrinsic evil—that it is absolutely and unequivocally always prohibited:

Some acts, apart from the intention or reason for doing them, are always wrong because they go against a fundamental or basic human good that ought never to be compromised. Direct killing of the innocent, torture, and rape are examples of acts that are always wrong. Such acts are referred to as intrinsically evil acts, meaning that they are wrong in themselves, apart from the reason they are done or the circumstances surrounding them. (*U.S. Catechism for Adults,* 311)

III. Methods of Moral Formation – *Cognitio Aestimativa*

Another treasure of the Catholic moral tradition is that it acknowledges "heart knowledge" as well as "head knowledge." Indeed, empathy—our capacity to sense others' emotions and communicate information essential for survival through a certain look, a tone of voice, or body posture and that connects us to all sentient being— is acknowledged as the beginning of morality in the anthropology of Thomas Aquinas. The significance of empathy is also confirmed by present-day psycho-social developmental theory. The ability to empathize was the difference psychologist Samuel Oliner found between those who rescued Jews from the Nazis in WWII and those who did not. Psychologist Martin Hoffman's studies of the psycho-social development of children indicated that empathy is learned best when parents use benevolent, teaching approaches when disciplining their children, helping them to imagine, think about, and reflect on the experience of the person who was wronged. Empathy requires that we see the other as our fellow human being—one who is created in God's image and likeness with inviolable dignity.

Theologian Johann Baptist Metz referred to the passion and death of Christ as a "dangerous memory" because it is a constant reminder to Christians that God is on the side of the tortured and the oppressed. As we fearful Christians see photos from Abu Ghraib, and hear the reports of the redefinition "waterboarding is not torture," we should heed the words of one who suffered through the heinous persecution of Communist Eastern Europe but yet taught:

These events are a warning to those who, in the name of political realism, wish to banish law and morality from the political arena.... It is by uniting their own suffering for the sake of truth and freedom to the suffering of Christ on the Cross that humanity is able to accomplish the miracle of peace and is in a position to discern the often narrow path between the cowardice which gives in to evil and the violence which, under the illusion of fighting evil, only makes it worse. *(John Paul II, World Day of Peace, "No Peace without Justice, No Justice without Forgiveness," 2002)*

Indeed, the perpetration of the violence of torture, "under the illusion of fighting evil, only makes it worse"! *Mea Culpa!*

Dawn M. Nothwehr, O.S.F., Ph.D.
Associate Professor of Christian Ethics, Catholic Theological Union
Chicago, IL

Faithfulness in an Age of Torture

Writing against torture strikes me as an absurd and troubling task. Something must have gone horribly wrong if it is necessary to criticize something as obviously immoral as torture. Torture, like child molestation, is simply wrong, deeply immoral, sick, and abhorrent. What else is there to say? And yet the ugly truth is that we as a people have failed to end our government's embrace of torture. There are of course exceptions, but many of us need to come clean: we have failed as citizens and sinned against God in acts of omission.

I use the word *failed* rather than *been defeated* because to date we have not even managed to establish ourselves as a serious opposition. As depressing as our failure is, even worse is the reason for our failure. Americans, by and large, have simply not been interested in stopping torture. If this sounds harsh, consider how loud those fighting against illegal immigration have been. Ironically, while they have been mobilizing and refining their message to one of "law and order," our legal system has been manipulated to accommodate the practice of torture. The key to explaining this irony lies in the words "national security." We live, we are told, in a different age, an age of terror that requires new thinking about how we treat non-citizens, especially those whom we suspect of posing a threat. The question now is whether we have become so fixated on preserving our security that we have lost touch with our deepest convictions.

In our legal system's accommodation of torture, we have witnessed the law being manipulated to serve duplicity and heinous wrongs. Throughout this debate officials in the executive branch have insisted that the United States has a policy against torture. This should come as no surprise since an argument for a policy of torture would sound like something out of a fantasy novel or some gruesome chapter of medieval history. Rather than attempting to defend torture, the administration has renamed certain practices of torture as "enhanced interrogation techniques."

The most well-known practice is that of causing a prisoner to fear he is being drowned, so-called waterboarding. The distinction between different forms of interrogation is a legitimate and important one, but this administration has failed to maintain this distinction in practice and as a matter of legal policy. The consequences of the failure to maintain a strong distinction between interrogation and torture can be seen in the lawless environments found at Abu Ghraib and Guantanamo. These are cases that have been brought to light and received considerable media attention. We also know that much is hidden from the light of day. The Bush Administration continues to make use of a network system of secret prisons. Because prisoners held in secret disappear from the outside world, even from the Red Cross, they are at the mercy of their captors, who have demonstrated their willingness to torture. This administration has also intentionally transferred prisoners to governments that are strongly suspected of torturing, such as Egypt and Saudi Arabia. In these four areas— redefining torture, permitting or promoting lawless prison environments, holding prisoners in secret, and transferring prisoners to nations suspected of torturing—the administration is guilty of great moral wrongs that have divided us politically and harmed our standing in the world.

In offering this criticism I feel the need to confess my own guilt for failing to condemn these practices as loudly as possible as soon as they came to my attention. Why have I and so many others failed to act? For some the answer is that they failed to see torture as an abhorrent practice on par with genocide and child molestation. For many of us, however, our failure is more complicated. When we witness a news report on torture many of us identify torture as abhorrent, but rather than acting, we often turn away in horror and disgust. To complicate matters further, once we have turned away, we tend to become ashamed of our turning away which then serves further to avert our attention, commitments, and actions. I am suggesting that our revulsion (and guilt) may ironically hinder us from acting to stop evil. The solution is not to prevent our revulsion or guilt but to find the courage to confront the evil. For Christians, God's abiding power and presence is a gift that empowers us to confront the revolting truth of our government's embrace of torture as well as our failure to do so in the past.

It is crucial that we come to terms with our moral failings because the fight against torture is not over. This administration appears determined to continue to make use of secret prisons and allied countries. In both cases we have good reason to worry that torture will continue to be used. Indeed, the disappearing of persons is itself a form of torture that should be condemned as such.

If we are to sustain the fight against torture, our reasons must be compelling. How should we respond when others argue that torture is wrong generally but that it cannot be ruled out completely because in some emergency it may save the lives of innocent civilians? Here one can surely draw on prudential reasoning to point out the unreliability of information gained through torture, but this is not the first answer for Christians. Our answer starts with the God of grace, the God of the cross who was tortured to death and offered forgiveness to the bitter end. Jesus is the Prince of Peace who calls us to a way of peace, even at the price of suffering. We are called to love our neighbors as ourselves and to pray for our enemies. For some, nothing else needs to be added. For those of us who believe that on rare instances war is justified, it is incumbent that we stipulate why the violence of war is to be limited, why civilians are to be protected, and why even prisoners are to be treated with respect. We must insist upon the basic conviction that prisoners, despite being suspected or even convicted of terrorism, remain our fellow human beings. To fail to remember their humanity is to invite great evil. In this age of torture we have learned the hard lessons of how evil corrupts the good, of how our best efforts, even our heroic efforts, can be twisted into abhorrent acts.

The grace of God frees us to see and act on the truth. Many of us have failed to dissent from our government's embrace of torture. Our failure, however, need not be the last word. Even now God calls us to raise our voices. To do otherwise is to permit torture in our name, to allow our nation to become a symbol of hypocrisy, and to betray our faith. We should take confidence in God's grace, repent of our sins, and respond with renewed fortitude to abolish torture.

David True
Associate Professor of Religion, Wilson College
Chambersburg, PA

An Islamic Perspective on Torture

In an effort to characterize the Muslim view on torture, let us consider a recorded statement of the Prophet Muhammad (peace be upon him) who said:

> A person should help his brother, whether he is an oppressor or is being oppressed. If he is the oppressor, he should prevent him from continuing his oppression, for that is helping him. If he is being oppressed, he should be helped by stopping the oppression against him.

Islam is a tradition that highly values the dignity of the human being and considers this dignity to be the essence of humanity. In the event that dignity is abused by torture, oppression or any other means, that humanity becomes questionable. According to the religion of Islam, God created human beings and honored them by making them His vicegerents on earth and responsible for taking care of the remainder of the creation in the Universe. The concept of vicegerency is repeatedly mentioned in the Holy Qur'an to emphasize the responsibility of the human being on this earth. The human being is commanded by God to do justice to His creation. The Holy Qur'an states that:

وَلَقَدْ كَرَّمْنَا بَنِي آدَمَ وَحَمَلْنَاهُمْ فِي الْبَرِّ وَالْبَحْرِ وَرَزَقْنَاهُمْ مِّنَ الطَّيِّبَاتِ
وَفَضَّلْنَاهُمْ عَلَى كَثِيرٍ مِّمَّنْ خَلَقْنَا تَفْضِيلًا الطَّيِّبَاتِ

"We have honored the sons of Adam; provided them with transport on land and sea; given them for sustenance things

good and pure; and conferred on them special favors, above
a great part of our creation." (Qur'an 17:70).

In this particular verse, God speaks about how much the human being is honored and valued in comparison to His other creatures. He was honored by being created to be the best of God's creation. The Angels protested the fact that they were not given the same level of honor; in fact, the leader of rebellious angels became Satan! Therefore, the human being needs to deeply contemplate this honor as it should be carried out into real life with responsibility.

This level of honor comes with tremendous responsibilities and duties toward all other creatures, in particular fellow human beings. What that means is that God would like to see this honor demonstrated to His entire creation. What that entails is dealing with others with dignity and as humanly as possible in all kinds of circumstances. This is a real test for those who violate the dignity of human beings by torturing and humiliating them in a way that clearly contradicts the basic understanding of this honor.

We have seen so many people abuse and violate this attribute which was bestowed on us by God himself, and as a consequence they are violating God's command. This happens when consciousness of God is weakened and people forget that they themselves might one day be caught in a similar situation.

Islam considers all humans as one family created from one source. If these torturers realize that they are torturing their own brothers and sisters, they would never think of doing such a terrible act.

Islam perceives the rights of the human being from the viewpoint of this honor as well as a vicegerent on this earth. These two concepts clearly describe how the human being should be treated in all circumstances, including at a time of war.

Islam strongly encourages its followers to practice the utmost compassion and mercy at the time when the individual, group, or state has the power and the upper hand. In these kinds of situations, Islam expects those in power to be just and to practice their power with justice and compassion.

Fourteen hundred years ago, the Prophet of Islam instructed his Companions to be just and deal with their enemy with mercy and compassion. He forbade them from torturing any individual. And in fact, ordered them to ensure that those who are in their custody are well fed and taken care of properly. A great example on this prophetic teaching is as follows:

> The Prophet (peace and blessings be upon him) passed by a prisoner who was in chains, and he called out, "O Muhammad, O Muhammad!" He came to him and said, "What is the matter?" He said, "I am hungry, feed me. I am thirsty, give me water." The Prophet (peace and blessings be upon him) commanded that his needs should be met. (Narrated by Muslim). And no doubt medical treatment is what a sick person needs.

In another Qur'anic verse. God says:

قَوْفَ مْكُضَعْعَبَ عَفَرَرَ وَ ضِرْلَأَ فَىئَلَخَ يِذَلَأ وَهَوَ
عُيِرِسَ كَبَرَ نَإِ مْكُاتَآ آَم يِف مْكُوَلْبَيِلَ تِاَجَرَدَ ضِعْبَ
مٌيِحَرَ رٌوفُغَلَ هُنَإِوَ بِاَقِعْلَا

"It is He Who hath made you (His) agents, inheritors of the earth: He hath raised you in ranks, some above others: that He may try you in the gifts He hath given you: for thy Lord is quick in punishment: yet He is indeed Oft-forgiving, Most Merciful." (Qur'an 6:165).

In this verse, God again emphasized the concept of the human being as an agent of God on this earth. The human being is assigned with higher responsibilities than the other creations, so those who are more privileged with power and wealth should be humble and considerate to others because God is testing them with these bounties.

This honor of responsibility which is bestowed on human beings requires great vigilance toward all of God's creatures, including fellow beings. To make someone as an agent act on your behalf means that there is a huge level of trust, confidence and honor and this trust should clearly be reflected in the honoree's behavior. It also indicates that the agent should execute his/her responsibility with utmost justice and transparency. This responsibility also entails giving greater attention toward those who are weak and cannot exercise their right. On the other hand the agent has the power to exploit this weakness and the state of the powerless.

Torture is opposed by Islam not only because it negatively impacts the dignity of the human being, but it also contradicts the notion of establishing justice on earth. This is the most crucial value following the belief in God. Islam emphasizes justice even when one is overwhelmed with hate and malice. God commanded the believers to never let their anger and abhorrence of a people cause them to deviate from justice, and asks us to fear Him and apply justice whether the person is a friend or an enemy, because justice is next to piety.

As far as the prisoners are concerned, Islam always treats prisoners with dignity and respect, and categorically opposes the torturing of captives and prisoners. It is regarded as a violation of justice and human dignity, and abuses of the concept of vicegerency, mentioned earlier.

The Prophet of Islam, Rahmat al-Alameen (who is described in the Qur'an as the "mercy to the Universe"), showed more mercy in his dealings with criminals who came to him voluntarily admitting their crimes. He asked them to repent and seek forgiveness from God.

The Prophet also emphasized the rule of Presumption of Innocence and affirmed this through his sayings and practice. Fourteen hundred years ago, the Prophet said: "Prevent punishment in case of doubt." What this tells us is that the evidence obtained through torture, or any way against the will of the human, has a doubtful status. Therefore, punishment should not be given on the basis of such doubtful evidence. We should also learn from this prophetic tradition that forcing prisoners or the accused to confess is legally unacceptable and morally wrong.

Islamic law is very clear on the issue of conviction. It should be based on confidence that the accused is guilty of wrongdoing, and there is no doubt or reasonable probability of innocence. Therefore, if there is any doubt, the case should be settled in favor of the accused person. This particular principle is based on the saying of the Prophet Muhammad: "Prevent punishment in case of doubt. Release the accused if possible, for it is better that the ruler be wrong in forgiving than wrong in punishing" (Al-Saleh). This Hadith is telling us that if the judge was not satisfied by the evidence presented before him or her and has reasonable doubt, then he should decide that the accused is not guilty.

There is no room in human dignity for torture. There is no room – we condemn torture. Islam condemns torture. Fourteen hundred years ago, the Prophet of Islam said the people that have the greatest chastisement on the Day of Judgment and in Hell are the people who tortured – that is the teaching of our Prophet (peace be upon him). We cannot accept torture.

In conclusion, it is clear that Islam has brought an unprecedented wealth of human and spiritual values to the people who have interacted with true Islam. Primary among these values was the knowledge and certainty that God Almighty bestows the gift of dignity upon every human being. It is an unqualified and unconditional gift, freely offered to the pious and sinful alike, irrespective of gender, religion, race, social status, age, power, etc. It is offered without restriction, both in times of peace or times of war.

Mohamed Elsanousi
Director of Communications & Community Outreach
Islamic Society of North America
Washington, DC

American Evangelicalism Repudiates Torture

The American faith narrative repudiates torture under all circumstances and without exception. To acquiesce our moral underpinning in the name of security renders in the hands of our enemies the very victory for which they yearn. Our nation's faith community stands committed to a value system authenticated via mores and standards that stand without reproach, unconditionally and in all circumstances. No other community embodies prophetic and moral standing against torture as does the faith family.

As a result of religious convictions, many suffered imprisonment, torture, and death. Correspondingly, the faith body in the twenty-first-century American experience must contextualize the moral narrative against such an egregious assault on civility and, above all, morality. From both a prophetic and justice platform, the practice of torture does not coalesce with the ethos of the American heritage.

Prophetically, evangelicals must, in lieu of our Life thread, address this issue in the same framework of life preservation as we address other relevant items in the social-political-cultural landscape. As a member of the steering committee of Evangelicals for Human Rights, I am troubled by evangelicals who embrace a pro-life platform yet refuse to address life issues outside the womb such as torture and cruel punishment.

In addition, some argue that waterboarding and other techniques applied to non-Americans does not violate the aforementioned commitment. Christians must disagree. Our values do not carry an American-centric disclaimer. Application of our ethos must transcend boundaries and cultures.

From a practical perspective, the great biblical Golden Rule and popularly embraced dictate tells us to do unto others what we would want done unto us. Such simplicity should guide us in our domestic, foreign, and justice policies. Is torture ever justified? Are there any moral absolutes? Are some of our values beyond compromise? Let the oracles of righteousness and justice articulate a message that protects our nation from terrorism. Not just physical but spiritual, moral, and intellectual.

Rev. Samuel Rodriguez
President, National Hispanic Christian Leadership Conference
Sacramento, CA

A Personal Reflection on the Use of Torture by Our Government

Three of the Ten Commandments call us to reverence human life and to respect the rights of others: "no killing, no adultery, and no stealing." Humankind is of infinite value to the Creator. Jesus underscores the radical dimension of this truth in his Sermon on the Mount: "Love your enemies, and pray for those who persecute you in order that you may be children of your Father in heaven." (Matthew 5:44-45a).

Think about it. Loving our enemies and praying for those who persecute us is telling evidence of our relationship to God. Jesus adds great weight to his command by continuing, "for if you love those who love you, what reward have you? Do not even the tax-gatherers do the same?" (Matt. 5:46). Note that Jesus does not question the reality of having enemies; in fact, he promises persecution for those who incarnate the Kingdom ethic. He makes it clear that loving only those who reciprocate that love does not distinguish those who claim to follow Jesus from those who do not. To love only those who love us reflects the way of the world, not the Kingdom of God.

Followers of Jesus are called to love their enemies, and to love someone is to look out for their welfare, to have compassion and concern for their happiness and well-being. This has significant relevance to the issue of torture. To personally engage in acts of torture, to oversee others who inflict torture, to affirm or participate in the torture of other persons is a blatant violation of a reverence for humankind.

No word characterizes the life and ministry of Jesus more clearly than compassion. Compassion is love in action. At her best, the church is a community of compassion. Matthew Fox, in *A Spirituality Named Compassion* (Winston Press, 1971), says that "compassion is not knowing about the suffering and pain of others. It is, in some way, knowing that pain, entering into it, sharing it and tasting it insofar as that is possible." We are not simply called to know that others suffer, to assess the painful situation in which they may be; we are to feel the other's feelings. And not only to feel the other's feelings, but to act on behalf of the other.

Unfortunately, we normally reserve compassionate concern for those closest to us like our friends and families. Jesus' call to love our enemies challenges the very structures of our social relationships. Over and over again in the Scriptures, Jesus challenged or ignored the social barriers of his day that marginalized and even dehumanized others so that he could love those often deemed so repulsive as to be characterized as less than human. He ate with sinners, invited himself into the house of a tax collector, publicly associated with those deemed immoral. He used as illustrations of faith such groups as the Samaritans and the Romans who were "outsiders" to the faith. In so doing Jesus reverenced those who were scorned because of their social status, their moral acts, or their ethnicity or race.

I restate a previous assertion: Our relationship to God is characterized by our relationship to others, those who are different than we, even our enemies. Could it be that the more we reverence others is indicative of the way we reverence God? The more humanly we treat others, the more human we become?

The issue of torture as the violation of God's infinite valuing of humankind and the explicit command of Jesus to "love our enemies, and pray for those who persecute us," is diverted by the use of labels. Designating others as "terrorists," "enemy combatant," "threats to national security" dehumanizes persons and distracts us from thinking clearly about our identity as Christ followers. "National security" trumps Kingdom thinking.

As Christ followers we can not allow perceived or real threat to lead us to accept torture of real or perceived enemies for so-called "national security interests." Inflicting torture on others is a cruel violation of Jesus' mandate to love our enemies.

In his Sermon on the Mount, Jesus states that his presence has fulfilled all that was promised by the Old Testament law and prophets.

(Matt. 5:17). Allow one of those prophets, Amos, to speak to us on this question of torture and national security versus love for our enemies.

Amos's book opens with a series of judgments on different nations for their treatment of others. From the outset it is clear that although God is most closely associated with the people of Israel, God's sovereignty to judge the mistreatment of others is not limited by ethnicity or national boundary. God holds all nations accountable for their abusive treatment of others.

The summary of his pronouncements about God's judgment against those who fail to reverence human life, who mistreat the poor and vulnerable, and who abuse the less powerful is the call to "let justice roll down like waters and righteousness like an ever-flowing stream."(Matt. 5:24). God's justice throughout the Old Testament is meant to be a healing balm to troubled lands. Such healing balm cannot be applied discriminately or selectively to only certain people deemed desirable or deserving. Justice is meant to soothe the afflicted and wash away all that stands in the way of human dignity to be experienced by all people.

Jesus goes radically further than Amos's call for justice and shared human dignity. He commands that love characterize the Christian's attitudes and behaviors towards those deemed "enemies." His is not a call to compassion "in general," but a call to specifically love those who persecute us.

The implications are clear. As Christ followers, we are called to not only refuse to engage in the torturing of others, but to love those deemed to be our "enemies." This means a fundamental concern for their happiness and well-being. The concern therefore necessitates a strong voice of advocacy that government leaders cease the practice of torture or the enabling of other nations to engage in torture.

The issue for American Christians today is not whether we ourselves would torture another. The question is will we silently and with complicity allow our enemies to be tortured and humiliated, or will we love them by speaking out against the use of torture?

Maxie Dunnam
Chancellor, Asbury Theological Seminary
Wilmore, KY

Torture: A Jewish Perspective

Torture is described in Webster's as "the inflicting of severe pain to force information or confession, get revenge, etc." The very idea of "inflicting severe pain" pierces and then destroys the boundaries of decency in a civilized world. Such piercing creates fragility and vulnerability in the hearts of all that are aware of it. The fabric of the universe suddenly begins to tear into raggedy pieces and no one escapes the fright of realization that there may be no center, only raw violence. Everyone and everything feels naked.

During this period, known as the War on Terror, America has been guilty of using torture in incident after incident. Even assuming only a fraction of the allegations of America's use of torture are true, and many certainly are, this country cannot engage in any acts that place us at the lowest common denominator of human morality. American soldiers should not pour phosphoric liquid on detainees or force groups of male prisoners to masturbate themselves while being photographed and videotaped or arrange naked male captives in a pile and then jump on them. The very notion of using extraordinary rendition, or moving detainees from American supervision to the supervision of a country that has fewer restrictions on torture, defies the imagination of what is minimally acceptable conduct in the universe of virtuous human actions. The tales of abuse are horrific and neither international law, Judaism, nor the American Constitution permit this kind of degradation of the human spirit and the human body.

Jewish tradition is not silent. While one could make the argument that there is some ambivalence in Biblical Judaism, as Judaism matured that ambivalence disappeared. Surely, our country has matured at least that much. The verses of the Bible go back and forth regarding the inflicting of pain. *Genesis* states that we are all made in the image of G-d but there are also numerous places in which G-d threatens to inflict severe examples of human pain if Israel does not repent her ways. As Judaism grew as a culture, as its understanding of the value of the human spirit evolved, the idea of using pain to gain information became less and less acceptable. The *Mishna*, the earliest rabbinic law code, states: "Thus, the human was created only as one individual, to teach us that anyone who destroys one soul is considered as if that person had destroyed the entire world." The Talmudic sage Ben Azzai said in response to the degradation of a human being, "Know who you are demeaning; G-d made 'him' in his own image." One does not torture someone created in the image of his or her G-d. Maimonides, the great medieval judge and scholar, in regard to the types of punishments a court may impose, concluded: "All these matters apply to the extent that the judge deems appropriate and necessary for the needs of the time. *In all matters* he shall act for the sake of heaven and not regard human dignity lightly.... He (the judge) must be careful not to destroy their dignity."

Bringing the matter of torture into today's world, the Israeli Supreme Court, recognizing that Israel lived in a world in which her very survival is threatened by terrorists who wish the annihilation of the Jewish state, still outlawed the use of torture in interrogations. In a clear and cogent statement the court concluded that forswearing inhumane means such as torture, even for honorable ends, "*is the destiny of democracy, as not all means are acceptable to it, and not all practices employed by its enemies are open before it.* Although a democracy must fight with one hand tied behind its back, it nonetheless has the upper hand. Preserving the rule of law and recognition of an individual's liberty constitutes an important component in its understanding of security. At the end of the day, they strengthen its spirit and its strength and allow it to overcome its difficulties."

The question of torture is not one that a democracy such as the United States should need to debate. Unfortunately, our actions in the world demand that we do hold this debate. As the leader of the world our example will guide the world. Our treatment of others, no matter how heinous their inclinations and crimes and how critical their perceived knowledge may be, and our respect for our own humanity will help determine the ethics of the world. We in America have great power and grave responsibilities. Piercing the boundaries of human decency is not the stuff of a great nation. At the end of the day, our capacity to do the right thing, to be a light among the nations, to love and respect the dignity of all human beings, will give us the spirit and the strength that allows us to prevail.

Rabbi Steve Gutow
Executive Director, Jewish Council for Public Affairs
Washington, DC

How to Read "An Evangelical Declaration against Torture"

The release of our statement, "An Evangelical Declaration against Torture: Protecting Human Rights in an Age of Terror," garnered considerable attention in mid-March 2007. However, surprisingly little of that attention went to themes that I think constitute the real significance of the document. Therefore, in this note I am including the statement itself as well as my own take on it as lead drafter.

How should one read "An Evangelical Declaration against Torture?"

First, read it as an expression of a sanctity-of-life ethic.

Our goal as drafters was to write an intellectually substantive, biblically rooted, theologically rich, definitively Christian treatment of U.S. detainee policy and practice in the war on terror. We sought to move beyond the kinds of brief declarations and slogans that often circulate on torture and other controversial moral issues, and instead tried to offer a serious analysis of a crucial set of moral concerns.

It was important to ground our stance in moral convictions that evangelical Christians (ought to) find non-negotiable. This was one reason why, as principal drafter, I grounded the declaration on the concept of the sanctity of every human life, a move that was never seriously questioned during the drafting process. One can hardly imagine a moral commitment that evangelicals (supposedly) take more seriously than this one. I personally believe that, rightly understood, the sanctity of life remains among the most powerful moral norms known to the church or to the human family. It is both clearly biblical and yet appealing to many outside of biblical faith. I am working on a book that revisits the sanctity of life concept in detail (Eerdmans, 2009). Here the declaration shows some early fruit of that work as it outlines key dimensions of a theologically rooted belief in life's sanctity and employs these as a beginning point for its treatment of torture.

Second, read it as a concretizing of a Christian human rights ethic that deals with a real area of moral vulnerability for our nation right now.

The sanctity of life becomes the grounding for a treatment of human rights in the declaration. Our treatment of human rights in section 2 of this document was vetted carefully by the drafting committee for its theological, ethical, and legal dimensions. I think it marks a significant step forward in the public articulation among evangelicals of a human rights ethic.

We argue that respect for human rights is fragile, and that it must include special vigilance on behalf of those whose rights are threatened. In this case, who would more likely qualify as vulnerable than a suspected terrorist moldering without charges and without public oversight in detention somewhere by a nation that still faces nightmares about 9/11?

We argue that even a fairly constrained understanding of human rights includes the right to security of person, which includes the right not to be tortured. We also make the critically important move of arguing that human rights cannot be cancelled, forfeited, or overridden. Most evangelicals—right, center, and left—say that they care about human rights. This is a concrete test of that affirmation. We know we really care about human rights when we care about the rights of our enemies and those we fear, not just ourselves or our friends.

Third, read it as a thrust in the intra-Christian argument about the concept of human rights.

We try to defuse the sometimes popular charge among academics that human rights is a modernist rather than Christian notion by exploring the rich but neglected Christian history of support for human rights. This is an important move that, so far, our critics have not challenged. This is good news, because Christian skepticism about the very validity of the concept of human rights can be quite damaging to Christian moral witness in public life.

Notice that in our treatment of human rights we never say that combatants have the right not to be killed, or that it is immoral to kill on the battlefield. Some have derided the text's "pacifist leanings," but this is demagoguery, or at least a blatant misreading. Though some pacifists found themselves able to sign it, ours is not a pacifist statement. I personally take the (widely held) position that while killing an enemy combatant on the battlefield can be justified, torture of a detained and disarmed prisoner cannot be similarly justified.

Fourth, read it as an argument in favor of the validity of both international law and domestic laws that ban torture.

Having built our argument first on sanctity, and then on human rights, in Section 5 of the Declaration we turn to a discussion of the various levels of moral responsibility that we have as individuals, churches, and governments to act to protect the human rights that we have been arguing are so important.

In Section 6 of the Declaration we try to show that bans on torture are abundantly clear and unequivocal in both international law and U.S. law. The fact that we cite international declarations, conventions, and treaties means that we are implicitly taking a stand in favor of honoring the significance and legitimacy of these instruments—which is noteworthy in its own right in light of conservative skepticism about international law. But we are always careful in the document to tie international obligations with U.S. law wherever that is possible.

Most of the drafters were theologians and ethicists rather than human rights lawyers and so this section turned out to need a bit of fine tuning once it saw the light of day in mid-March. We are grateful for the line-by-line refinements that various lawyers contributed to this section after its initial release. I learned from this process not just to appreciate international human rights and humanitarian lawyers but also that the United States had actually been edging away from its unequivocal support of international human rights treaties and conventions for some time, not just since 9/11—and that it is actually a mistake to now describe our nation as a leader in protecting human rights. Nothing I have heard has made me think that such an edging away from a strong stance on human rights by our government is anything other than a very bad idea, and one that ultimately weakens our international standing and role in the world.

Fifth, read it as praise of the Pentagon, and not as a slam on the Bush Administration.

One of the most important contributions of Section 6 of the Declaration is the appeal to the revised U.S. Army Field Manual. After a considerable struggle within the Pentagon, the most recent revision of this manual contains an admirably detailed rejection of many of the particular interrogation techniques that at least arguably crossed the line into torture. Some would like to have seen the Pentagon go further and explicitly ban, for example, the use of stress positions and sleep deprivation, but it has at least banned some of the most notorious acts that were authorized, or permitted, or occurred, despite not being permitted, after 9/11. Thus we are able to simplify our policy argument to ask flatly that all branches of the federal government should play by the rules instituted by the Pentagon without exception.

"Do as the Pentagon does" is hardly a radical statement, and yet we have still been on the receiving end of predictable criticism from the right wing of the political-religious landscape for our "attack on the Bush Administration."

When a Christian group such as our own drafting committee implicitly acknowledges that there has been a fissure within a particular administration, in which some have argued for respecting strict bans on torture and others have argued for loosening them, and we side with those who take the strict rather than loose stance, this is not an attack on a president, a party, or an administration. It is at least at one level an expression of support for those voices within that administration who have taken one view rather than another. We are glad that the more "strict constructivist" voices are gaining in strength in the latter days of the Bush Administration. We reject the idea that our criticism of other voices is a "religious left" slam on that same administration. This is one reason why a mainstream evangelical group like the National

Association of Evangelicals (NAE), with strong ties, for example, to the military chaplaincy, could endorse this statement.

Sixth, read it as a broadening of concern from torture to overall detainee policies and finally to the rule of law.

The drafters came to the conviction that opposition to torture must not be the entirety of our policy agenda. Many features of the Military Commissions Act of 2006, for example, come in for criticism in this document. The use of the CIA for detentions, interrogations, and extraordinary renditions to other countries, all placed *in principle* beyond the reach of citizen oversight, creates concerns that are related to torture but also distinguishable from it. One might say that the agenda of the document in this sense evolved from "ban torture" through "protect detainees" to end up with "protect the rule of law." These concerns are connected, of course. But many now join us in seeing that you cannot weaken constitutional protections anywhere without threatening them everywhere.

Seventh, read it as an expression of Christian discipleship.

One of the most distressing things about the predictable criticism the document received was the immediate translation of the statement into a "culture wars" paradigm—and indeed, into the "evangelical culture wars" of latter days. To criticize the use of torture is seen as a thinly veiled partisan attack on the Republican president of the United States. To criticize the use of torture is seen as a victory for Rich Cizik and the NAE over against James Dobson and his cohorts on the Christian Right.

All of this marks a sad degradation of evangelical moral discourse. Not to put ourselves in too lofty a crowd, but should we interpret Wilberforce as an anti-George III partisan? Was Bonhoeffer simply fronting for the Socialists? Was Solzhenitsyn just a CIA agent trying to bring down the Soviet regime? Should King be seen as one who used race as a wedge issue to elect a Democratic president in 1968? Is the evangelical movement against sex trafficking a hidden anti-globalization crusade secretly led by the Green Party?

What are Christians supposed to do who have actual *moral objections* to an action of their government? What I believe they should do is gather together to test their views in community, analyze the issue as best they can using the resources of the Christian tradition, and then offer a carefully and prayerfully crafted moral reflection that expresses dissent rooted in Christian conviction.

David P. Gushee
President, Evangelicals for Human Rights and Professor of Ethics, Mercer University
Atlanta, GA

Torture and the Christian Faith

I am among those who believe that a young adult Jew—who was tortured to death by a coalition of governmental and religious leaders—is God. Attempting to worship and to follow a victim of military torture does something to you. For one thing, it's impossible to think about torture in the same way, after bleeding, tortured, Jesus looks at you and declares, "I am the way, the truth, and the life." Christians are neither dispassionate nor neutral when it comes to torture. Jesus made us that way.

As Christians, we are accountable to a story that says, among other things, that there is something about God in Jesus Christ that made us look at him and (democracy in action!) with one voice cry, "Torture him!" And there is something about us that thought that the purpose of government is to provide us peace, justice, and security even if it must torture a rabbi and two thieves to do it. And there is something about Jesus, victim of torture, that made him look upon those who tortured him and say, "Father forgive, they don't know what they are doing."

Scripture is the lens through which Christians look at the world, the means by which we know the world is the world. Viewed through the lens of the story of Jesus, torture is an admission by the world that the world is still, for any of its alleged progress, the world. The world is where those in power calls the shots. The way to handle the differences, tensions, and disparities that abound in the world is to label a group of people as "enemy" or "evil" or "undemocratic" or "terrorist" while labeling ourselves and our self interest as aspects of "good," "homeland security," and "in defense of freedom." Such designation cultivates the self-understanding that enables us to torture those for whom Christ died without a twinge of conscience.

The narrative of Jesus' death teaches us that torture is what we Christians expect out of governments, be they democratic or otherwise. Call us cynical if you will but at least you can't say we are naïve. Violence is the result of worshiping anything other than the Trinity—God in which Father, Son, and Holy Spirit dwell in complete peace and fellowship with one another.

Most of our early Christian heroes were tortured to death— Stephen was stoned, Paul probably beheaded. More Christians around the world have been persecuted (and many of them tortured) in the twentieth century than in perhaps any previous time. Yet, in a perverse twist of history, Christians sometimes assumed the role of torturers. Some of the torturers at Abu Ghraib were good Methodist kids just obeying orders. Such are the results of switching stories from the one about the Savior who was tortured, to the one about the nation-state that can do no wrong because we are unjustly attacked, powerful, free, and democratic, and they are not.

Torture today is linked to the creation of the modern state. Thomas Hobbes first explained to us what the modern state is for: freedom. Although at first glance the modern nation seemed by many to be a dangerous threat to human liberty, Hobbes explained that the liberty granted by the state was the only liberty worth having:

> Every citizen retains as much liberty as he needs to live well in peace, enough liberty is taken from others to remove the fear of them.... To sum up: outside the commonwealth is the empire of passions, war, fear, poverty, nastiness, solitude, barbarity, ignorance, savagery; within the commonwealth is the empire of reasons, peace, security, wealth, splendor, society, good taste, the sciences, and good-will.[1]

This is the story that now holds us captive, a definition of reality that no longer requires argument. We have irreversibly given over all

---

1 Thomas Hobbes, *On the Citizen,* ed. and trans. Richard Tuck (Cambridge University Press, 1998), pp. 115-116.

power to the state. We are told that by allowing the state to define the world, we shall have security. The state is the only means of securing human harmony and security. Outside the state, there is only "passions, war, fear, poverty, nastiness, solitude, etc." While our past century has proved Hobbes's argument to be a lie—more people have been killed in the past century by their own governments than have been killed even in war—for most of us Hobbes's is the only story we've got and, as we have shown repeatedly, we will defend it with murderous intensity.

While I can understand how members of other faiths would have trouble believing that a tortured-to-death Jew from Nazareth is the King of the World and that his Kingdom of peace is more real than Caesar's realm (since they have heard professing Christians defend and excuse torture as a tool of national security), the Christian faith is a rich resource for countering our tendencies toward torture. The God who meets us in Jesus Christ is the God in whom no justification for torture can be found. I mention just two relevant aspects of Christian believing: *Jesus Christ died for all and all of us, including the followers of Jesus, are sinners.* I know of no orthodox Christian who would challenge either of those assertions.

Jesus Christ died for all. "God so loved the world that he gave his only begotten Son.... God sent the son into the world not to condemn the world but that the world through him might be saved" (John 3:16). Even if you don't know what we mean by "save" you can't miss "the world" in this statement from the Gospel of John. Jesus Christ is God's verdict on all of humanity. It is God's will that all be saved (1 Timothy 2:4). There was a time when Christians so vibrantly believed this that we sent missionaries to places like Iraq in order to tell them the news that Jesus Christ died for everybody, including them. Now we send an army to Iraq to force the Iraqis to believe that democracy, as we practice it, will save them. Go figure.

When we ceased to be driven by the conviction that God values each and every human being, no matter that human being's earthly status, nationality, or ideological stance, the door was opened for torture. I think this is part of what Tolstoy meant when he said that, "Without God anything is possible." When our actions are judged by no greater arbiter than our own conscience, expect the worst of us. Christians try to look at people in much the same way that God looks at people. When we let the modern nation state define people and set the limits for our behavior, we're in trouble because the sweeping, embracing implications of Jesus Christ are whittled down to Caesar's definitions.

All are sinners. St. Paul is clear that all of us, every one of us, particularly those of us who consider ourselves to be God's people, are in rebellion against God. We are sinners. This once was one of the most widely attested, exuberantly celebrated beliefs of Christians. Jesus Christ died forgiving the very sinners who put him to death. He was put to death by a consortium of people, all of whom believed that they were doing the right and good thing in crucifying him, many of whom believed that they were doing a godly thing in murdering Jesus. Sin for Christians is personal and corporate, individual and social, a matter of what we do and who we are and it is the one thing that links us in solidarity with everyone else. In fact, to be a Christian is increasingly to learn to that you are a more wretched sinner than you thought before you became a Christian. You come to learn that your sin is not just in the bad things that you do that you know that you shouldn't, but rather sin is a constant inclination of the human heart, the way we always put ourselves first, the tendency always to ascribe better motives to our actions than they deserve, the way we keep organizing the whole world around ourselves, the way we self-righteously divide the world into two classes of people—those who deserve torture and we who can do unto others as we please. For most of us, our sin is not in that we tortured other people but rather our sin is that we asked our government to provide us peace, justice, and security no matter what it cost.

This says to me that as a Christian clergyman I've got my hands full encouraging fellow Christians to see more clearly, to love more dearly, and to follow more nearly the tortured one whom we call Savior of the World. He commanded us not simply to treat our enemies with tolerance and justice, which would have been hard enough. Jesus ordered us to *love* our enemies and *to pray for those who abused us.* We can't worship Jesus without obeying Jesus and, when it comes to torture, our obligations as Christians are clear. While I'm in no position to speak for other faiths, when it comes to the peculiarly Christian faith, condemnation of torture is a non-negotiable ethical demand. And the committing of torture by anyone, or the defense of torture for any reasons, is a horrifying revelation of something badly amiss in the soul of the torturer.

A couple of days after 9/11, a TV reporter interviewed a couple who stood by a fence at "ground zero." They were clutching a photograph of their beloved daughter who had been in the World Trade Center on that day. One could see the fear and the growing sense of hopelessness upon their faces.

The reporter interviewed them. Then the reporter concluded with, "Well, er, this weekend, I guess you'll be going to your place of worship and I hope that you will find some comfort there."

The mother replied, "No. We won't be going to our place of worship this weekend. We're Christians. And a big part of our faith is forgiveness. And frankly, we're just not ready to hear about that yet." And I, as a preacher, took some comfort in knowing that even in America, there was one woman who really knew the perils and the promise of worshiping Jesus.

William H. Willimon
Bishop, United Methodist Church, North Alabama Conference
Birmingham, AL

The Truly Human Response to a World Gone Mad

Nothing can be further from God than that which has been made accursed.
—Simone Weil

The images of torture that have managed to surface in the public media, hardly inclusive of the breadth of the practice I'm sure, reveal acts inflicted upon others that are not only degrading and painful, but also life-threatening. It has come to public attention that persons with varying degrees of accused guilt or innocence are being held in secret prisons without any representation, advocacy, or even the illusion of due process. They are cut off from their families and friends with absolutely no recourse, absolutely no power. This, in itself, is a form of torture.

As a person of faith, the Christian faith in particular, I am not only distressed and grieved by the revelation of these acts against humanity by the United States (and other countries and groups). I am disgusted, sickened, and outraged. Though I hasten to add my outrage is not of a surprised nature. When all of life is treated as a commodity, when the tendency of culture is to use any means necessary to produce whatever we want as efficiently and cheaply as possible, when the value of human life is measured more by cost-benefit analysis than by the inherent worth of persons *as* human beings, when the rhetoric and policy of nations, churches, and other interest groups seem to emphasize what divides and excludes human beings rather than what connects and unifies, it seems that torture is simply taking things to the logical end: the person who is tortured becomes one more means to an end, one more product to be consumed and thrown away, one more leper to confine to the tombs.

The Christian faith provides as good a corrective to this trajectory as any. Theologian Hans Urs von Balthasar puts it this way:

> What distinguishes … Christian faith … is this: the hand of the loving Father, who grasps the fumbling child, is the hand of a *human* you. The hand of our neighbor: "'Who is neighbor to him who fell among robbers?' He answered, 'He who showed mercy on him.' And Jesus said to him 'Go and do likewise'" (Lk. 10:36 ff.). The fact that God's hand is the hand of *one particular* fellow human being makes of the hand of every fellow human being something quite new…. Only where God is person is the human being taken seriously as a person.[1]

For Christians, God has come into the world as a *human*. "And the Word became flesh and lived among us … full of grace and truth." (John 1:14). We believe that the mystery of the Incarnation—the claim that Jesus of Nazareth was fully God and fully human—not only teaches us about who God is, but also shows us what it means to be "fully human." In Jesus Christ we see:

> The revelation of the *homo verus*, the true and complete human being … a human being in whom, as a matter of fact, all the characteristics of true human nature are present…. And since the central core of this true humanity is Jesus' great love for human beings, we assert that love exists and that not only does evil make its presence felt on this earth, but we are also enfolded in love … human beings have been able to see love on earth, to know what they are, and what they can and should be.[2]

---

1   Hans Urs von Balthasar, "The Personal God," in *The von Balthasar Reader*, eds. Medard Kehl and Werner Löser, trans. Robert J. Daly, S.J., and Fred Lawrence (New York: The Crossroad Publishing Company, 1997), 193-194.

2   Jon Sobrino, *Jesus the Liberator: A Historical-Theological View*, trans. Paul Burns and Francis McDonagh (Maryknoll, NY: Orbis Books, 1993), 229-230.

If we claim to know and follow the truly human one, Jesus Christ, then we know what we "can and should be:" our capacity and our goal is to be like Christ, to be and to become more fully, truly *human*.

The core of "true humanity" is love for other human beings. I can think of nothing further from love than the infliction of torture upon another human being. I can think of nothing that separates us from our own capacity for being human more than the infliction of torture upon another human being. And I can think of nothing that strips another person of their own humanity more fully than being subjected to torture at the hands of another. In other words, torture is profoundly *dehumanizing* not only for those who are tortured, but also for those whose hands brandish torturing tools. To participate in or advocate for such dehumanizing behavior is in direct contradiction with the Christian faith.

I can already hear the questions being posed: What about the fact that others in the world inflict violence and seek to do us harm? What about the fact that others in the world do not share our value of human life? What practical good is it to speak of "love for other human beings" when those other human beings would just as soon blow themselves up—and us with them—if they had the chance? What about justice? These are natural questions to ask in a world gone mad with hatred, strife, and violence. If fear, self-protection, and vengeance are the primary guides in our response to these questions, then it is also natural to conclude that torture is not only acceptable but necessary in some cases. However, for those of us who seek to truly follow—and not just pay lip-service to—the truly human one, we will persistently and consistently take our stand with Jesus, who did not raise hand or sword to those who clearly had murderous intent. If we respond to violence and threat of violence with brutality and hatred, then we have sacrificed not only our humanity but also our faith in the power of God which was most fully revealed not through vengeance but through self-sacrificing love.

The question of justice becomes complicated by the overwhelming misconception that it has to do with "eye for an eye" retribution, together with the further misguided notion that justice has nothing to do with love. From a Christian perspective, "the Gospel makes no distinction between the love of our neighbor and justice."[3] When we are guided by the baser instincts of vengeance and when we have the power to exert those instincts through the means of torture, it may seem to us that we are acting within the realm of "justice." But the truth of the matter is that in so acting we could not be further from the justice of God.

An ancient concept of divine justice holds that "divinity, like humanity in its natural state, always carries its power of commanding to the extreme limit of possibility."[4] But the God who was revealed in Jesus does not exercise power to the extreme limit of possibility; rather, the justice of God is shown in restraint and renunciation of the exercise of power. That is to say, while it is *possible* for God to treat humankind as pawns, as "things"; while it is *possible* for God to inflict punishment on humankind that is equal to what is deserved, God has chosen to have mercy upon us, to become vulnerable to us, and even to call us "friends." (John 15:15). "The supernatural virtue of justice consists of behaving exactly as though there were equality when one is the stronger in an unequal relationship."[5] Without this loving, merciful behavior on the part of the "stronger" person, the "weaker" person loses personhood, passing into the state of matter and becoming like a "thing."[6] In order to be truly human, as revealed in Jesus, we will not simply do what is possible (power/strength); we will do what is just (loving). This means that we human beings who bear the image and likeness of God will show the kind of restraint of which we are capable. Quite frankly, this means that we will not reduce other human beings to the "state of matter" or treat them as "things" through the infliction of torture just because it is in our power to do so.

This kind of justice may seem impractical to many. It won't be the first time that this charge has been leveled against the Christian faith. In the end, to be human as Jesus Christ is human, is not about efficiency or practicality or might. To be truly human is to reflect more fully the image of the Creator whose divine love and justice was embodied in a vulnerability that led to the Cross. Standing in the shadow of the Cross,

---

3   Simone Weil, "Forms of the Implicit Love of God," in *Waiting For God*, trans. Emma Craufurd (New York: G.P. Putnam's Sons, 1951), 85.

4   Ibid., 88.

5   Ibid., 87.

6   Ibid.

one would think that we would recognize our shame and collusion in the torture of human persons—in the torture of the truly human one, Jesus. I refuse to be one of those who call themselves Christian, feel smug about my awareness of guilt on Good Friday, and then do nothing in the face of the continued torture of bodies and souls. Instead, I stake my claim on the "foolishness" of the Cross, the "foolishness" of God's justice, the "foolishness" of God's love. (1 Corinthians 1). I believe that only this foolishness bears hope for the world; only this foolishness offers any real way out of the degradation revealed in photographs of U.S. soldiers collaring and treating like dogs those whom they are charged with imprisoning. My prayer is that our country—and our world—will have the faith and courage to become more and more "foolish," more Christ-like, more truly human.

Rev. Ginger E. Gaines-Cirelli
Pastor, Capitol Hill United Methodist Church
Washington, DC

www.ingramcontent.com/pod-product-compliance
Lightning Source LLC
Chambersburg PA
CBHW060649290526
45793CB00001B/468